DEAR God

by MARGE CALDWELL

TABLE
OF CONTENTS

CONTENTS

First Edition 1997

Editor – Angela Thomas Guffy

Design & Photography – TRiBe! DeSiGN, Houston, Texas

ISBN 0-9657223-0-9

DEDICATED
TO CHUCK

My precious husband of 60 years,
who has always been there with love, encouragement,
and support.

preface

I have been privileged to speak at Women's Retreats across the nation. After a session is concluded, the lights are dimmed, and I go to the microphone and talk to God about what I've just seen and heard. At one session, I will talk to Him from the perspective of a lonely single girl. Another time I might be a young housewife or a mother-in-law. One day a lady asked me for a copy of my prayers. Of course I didn't have one, so she said, "Please write those down!" But you see, I was too busy counseling on Monday and Tuesday, and traveling each weekend, so I forgot!

One night we had dinner with Bonita and Steve Seelig. We were discussing this very topic, and Steve asked me to put my prayers in writing. "I'm too busy," I said. But the spark he ignited became a flame! I had no idea how I could crowd writing into a busy schedule, but God arranged that for me. In a few weeks, I found myself in the hospital with an uneven heartbeat -- and I was there for a month!

A strange but wonderful thing took place. Every morning for ten days I woke up at 4 a.m. and had a chapter in my mind. I would quickly write it down. My husband, Chuck, nearly fainted one night at the beginning of this episode when he awoke and found me feverishly writing. "What are you doing?" he asked. "I'm writing my book, Chuck!" I wish you could have seen his face. "You're supposed to be sick," he laughed. I kept on writing.

Some of the chapters are personal chapters where I share my own experiences with you. Other chapters are prayers by other people who have crossed my path in the last few years.

My hope and desire is that through this book, our wonderful Savior, Jesus, might touch your heart and heal your hurts! May He bring you joy too . . . there's much laughter here!

MARGE

HAPPY Birthday

Dear God,

I would have never dreamed in a million years that I would be in the hospital on my birthday. What a dismal place to celebrate, but a good place to be when you're not running on all four cylinders. In the hospital, just like at summer camp, we're supposed to complain about the food. I wasn't very "cool" because I thought the food was good. But Lord, I'll tell You what wasn't "cool." At 5 a.m. every morning, in came a large blustery, nurse who wanted to take my blood. After a few mornings of that, I thought I'd surely need a transfusion. Next came a group of nurses who wanted to take my vital signs. Well, at 5 a.m. my signs weren't vital, and I wanted to tell them they'd get more vital around 8 or 8:30. Can You imagine taking a person's weight while it's still dark outside? I'd hear those scales squeaking down the hall and think, "Oh no!" Wearily, I'd crawl on. It's bad enough to tell a patient they've gained three pounds in the daytime, but in the middle of the night? How depressing!

Still, so many beautiful things happened. I was allowed to go home late in the afternoon of my birthday. But that morning, five precious nurses came to visit with a "birthday cake." Now that was one of the most beautiful cakes I've ever had -- even though it was a cinnamon roll with a tiny candle in it. They sang "Happy Birthday," and of course, I cried.

My friend Beverly sang "My Tribute" to me as a special birthday gift. We all had tears running down our cheeks. There was never a more thrilling testimony than Beverly singing "How Can I Say Thanks," while her husband, Jack, lay critically ill in ICU.

People up and down the hall were listening. They all knew her circumstances. How awesome You are, God, to give Your children such strength and courage in times of distress or trouble.

I keep remembering how You've told us that You will never leave us or forsake us. All through Your Word, You give us that promise. One of the most precious is found in Deuteronomy 31:6. We can't tell You enough how grateful we are to know that You're always there. **Oh, thank You God, that we can love You in joy and also in pain. Thank You.**

ON BEING
Available to God

Dear God,

Today I've been thinking about that wonderful Scripture, Romans 8:28, "And we know that in all things God works for the good of those who love Him, who have been called according to His purpose." That scripture is so fabulous -- it doesn't say all things are good, it just says all things work together for the good of those who love You and are faithful. Lord, it is so exciting to know for sure that You take the bad things that happen in our lives, turn them around, and make them work for the best. I think about some of the mistakes we make and the silly things we do, and how You turn it all around and make it good, inspite of us!

The best example I associate with this scripture happened many years ago. You must have been very discouraged with me about the reaction I had that day. I never will forget it, I was teaching a young married's class. They were the cutest couples and we had so many little babies -- we had 18 babies in one year! Chuck said, "For heaven's sake, Marge, don't drink after any of them!" My soul, we played Mama and Papa and enjoyed every minute of it.

Back in those days we did a lot of visiting before Houston got so large. Every Monday, Thelma (the President of our class) and I would go visit the people who had visited our class the day before. That particular Monday, I told Thelma I could go visit with her until noon and perhaps we could grab a hamburger, but I had a one o'clock appointment that afternoon I had to keep. That was fine and we started our day. We visited several people and stopped for lunch, and Thelma said, "Oh, Marge, instead of eating this hamburger, let's go and visit one more person. She's on my heart and I feel like we need to go visit her." I said, "Now Thelma, I told you I had to be gone by one o'clock." God, You know how I felt inside, I felt like I wasn't being very spiritual. I told Thelma she was laying a guilt trip on me because I didn't want to go visit another person. Anyway, she insisted and I gave in, even though my attitude wasn't very good.

We knocked on the door and finally a young lady, Marilyn, came to the door, and she was crying. I introduced myself and Thelma told her we were from First Baptist Church. She burst out crying even more, and asked us to come in. We asked her what was wrong. She said she had been down on her knees by her bed praying for God to send somebody to help her. She was upset and didn't know which way to turn. Marilyn explained that her husband had left her that morning even though she was seven months pregnant. He said he wasn't coming back and she believed him. Thelma and I felt so sorry for her and we were glad that we were there. It was obvious we were supposed to be there and I thought, "If Thelma looks at me, I'll whip her!" We talked for a while and I asked Marilyn if she knew Jesus Christ as her Savior. Had she ever asked Him to come into her heart? She answered "No," and Thelma and I had the privilege of opening the Bible and telling her how she could be saved. That day, right about noon, Marilyn asked Jesus Christ to come into her heart. We all loved on each other and had the most wonderful time.

We decided to invite Marilyn to our class because she was the same age as the other ladies in the class and we wanted to help her grow in her faith. The way that class took care of her was so sweet. They gave her baby clothes and everything she needed for her new baby. We had a wonderful time encouraging her in the last months of her pregnancy. The time came for her delivery, and still her husband didn't come back. Chuck and I went up to the hospital to be Mama and Papa, and Marilyn gave birth to a sweet little boy. It was so wonderful to see how the girls in the class surrounded her and took such good care of her. They even took turns baby-sitting for each other's children so they could help Marilyn until she was able to take care of herself.

The days passed and I wonder if You realize how good that

whole experience was for my class? They bonded together and they bonded with her -- we were like family. Marilyn had a wonderful time, except for the sadness she felt that her husband wasn't there to share her joy. Not long after this, we had a big party planned for all the couples. I asked Marilyn if she would call her husband, Bill, and ask him if he would come. She told me he couldn't stand Christians. She said, "He thinks they don't know how to have fun, and anyway, he hasn't been around the last six months." I told Marilyn the difference now was that we could pray for God to bring him. So, I challenged the girls and we all started praying earnestly that if Marilyn called him, he would come. One of the guys in the class called Bill, and God really answered our prayers -- he came! Of course, the guys in the class were so mad at the way he had acted toward Marilyn and the baby and the girls were absolutely disgusted with him. But we all promised not to let that show if he came.

Bill had the best time in the world and so did we! I called the hostess before the party started and said, "Honey, if you ever had a fun party, help this to be a fun party," and I told her why. She outdid herself! We laughed and had the time of our lives! Marilyn's husband was right at home with everybody. He came over to me and said very quietly, "Can I ask you to forgive me? I am so sorry about the way I have treated my wife and baby. I feel so bad about the way I've felt about Christians -- I've never had so much fun in my life and these guys are great! I love this bunch of people." As the days wore on, he came back to his wife and baby. They began to work on their relationship and things improved. Our class supported them and helped them grow spiritually, and Marilyn and Bill are happily married today.

God, thank You for showing me the difference between doing something good for You and doing the best for You. Of course, You know that I never got to the meeting that day, but who cares. The meeting I had planned to attend was something good, but this was the best! Help me to always know the difference, dear God, between good and best. As I have thought about this, I think it's funny how we lose sight of what is important. Lord, please make me available to what you want me to do everyday. Please make me available to what You want me to do. I make my little plans and don't want anyone to mess them up. I hold up my days for You to bless and think everything I'm doing is wonderful! When You have a different plan for me, I get frustrated. God help me to know the difference between a good thing and the best thing. Romans 8:28 is teaching me to be more flexible with You than I have been in the past. I love You so much Lord. Help me to always remember that class and what happened to precious Marilyn because two people -- one who listened to You, and the other one who was too busy. Thank You for Your wonderful care and for teaching us about flexibility. **Thank You for changing our plans, Lord. Thank You for today.**

YOUNG
Hearts Can Suffer

Dear God,

I want to talk to You today about children. We hear so much about teenagers and what a hard time they have. Today I'm thinking about the younger children, and how much they misinterpret what happens and what is said around them. I remember from the time I was two or three years old my Daddy would say things like, "I want a boy, and I got Marge." Or when he was around friends he'd complain, "I wanted to go play ball with her, but she wants to play with dolls," and "I wanted to go fishing, but she hates worms." When we're around little kids, we have to be careful what we say because they don't know we're kidding. They don't know how to interpret what adults say. They just take it at face value. When I was growing up, I thought there must be something wrong with me -- I should have been a boy. It really did something to me for quite a few years. I think about children in the world today -- all the dysfunctional and broken homes where the children are really the victims. I've seen some wonderful things happen to straighten those children out in our counseling center. I especially remember a little seven year-old girl, Courtney. Her parents brought her in to see me because she cried all the time. They had already seen their pediatrician and others to try and help her. They couldn't find anything physically wrong with her, so they brought her to the counseling center to see if she needed some type of psychiatric care. At school, Courtney would cry all the time and her teachers would have to send her home. She never could explain to them what she was crying about. They would question her to try to find some sort of pattern to it all, but they couldn't find anything.

Courtney was a darling little girl. She wore a cute little

outfit the day she came to see me. Her purse matched her clothes perfectly, as did the bow she wore in her hair. Her parents waited out in the foyer while Courtney and I talked. At first we did a lot of small talk, "How are you? . . . Darling, you look so pretty . . . I just love your purse." I tried to help her feel at ease and she responded sweetly to everything I said. Then I said, "Courtney, would you like to help me by telling me why you cry? She said, "I don't want to." I told her how much I wanted to help her -- there was nothing I'd rather do than help her stop crying. She said, "Do I have to tell you?" I told her she didn't have to, but I hoped she would say something to let me know why the tears flow all the time. She kind of snuggled up to me on the sofa and said, "I guess I have to tell you. My mommy and daddy are going to get a divorce." Well, I knew her mother and father, and I knew they weren't about to get a divorce. I told her it wasn't true but she insisted they were. I asked her why she was so sure they were going to divorce. She said, "My best friend Kathy lives three houses down from me. Her mommy and daddy got a divorce not long ago." I told her that didn't mean that her mother and daddy were going to, but she kept insisting. I asked her what made her so sure and she said, "Well, before Kathy's parents got divorced, they argued and fought. Her mom was crying all the time, and the father was slamming doors, and they called each other names. Then, they got a divorce!" I asked her what that had to do with her mom and dad. She said, "My mom and dad are doing the same thing! They argue all the time. He calls her bad names and she cries. They slam doors, and I know they're going to get a divorce!" I asked Courtney if she would mind sitting out in the foyer while I talked to her mom and dad for a few minutes. I asked her if I could share with them what she had told me. She agreed to let me, but didn't think it would do any good.

Courtney left the room and I motioned for her mother and father to come in. I told them I found out why their sweet little girl was crying all the time and they said, "For heaven's sake, what is it?" I told them word for word what she had said. The mother bowed her head and cried, and the father looked stunned. They put their arms around each other and said, "She's right, that's exactly what we've been doing for the last three or four months." They had been having financial problems and it had caused a strain on their marriage. One of their parents was very ill and in a nursing home, and it was an emotional strain. Instead of pulling them together, trouble had made them tense with each other, as well as unkind and unfair. They knew what Courtney had said was true. I told them she was absolutely convinced they were going to get a divorce because of what happened to Kathy's parents. I asked the mom and dad if I could call Courtney in and tell her what had been said. I asked them to promise never to argue or fuss in front of her again. They had to talk their problems out together, and most of all, promise Courtney that there would never be a divorce. She had to understand that their family was forever. I asked them if they were willing to that, and they were. Courtney came back in and sat down by her parents. I asked her parents to explain to her why they had been feeling so badly lately and why they had been so unkind to each other..

Oh, God, I know You were in the room with us and You saw that beautiful scene..I wish everybody could have seen it, Lord. I wish every thoughtless parent in the world could have seen this mother turn to her daughter, and say, "Courtney, I promise you from the bottom of my heart, as I'm promising God that even though your dad and I have been very unkind and unloving to each other, we really do love each other and we definitely are not going to get a divorce. We promise you that all of the arguing and ugliness that you've been seeing in our home for the last few months is going to stop. From this day on, with God's help, we're going to be the loving and kind parents that you deserve."

Then Courtney's dad put his arm around her and said, "Courtney, we love you so much and we love each other so much. We promise you, right here in front of Ms. Caldwell and in front of God, that we will never let this happen again. We will be kind and loving to each other and we will never argue or yell in front of you again. We ask you to forgive us and we know that you will. We're going to ask God to forgive us, and we know that He will. It's going to be a new day at our house, Courtney." She grabbed her dad and mom and they all three hugged each other and cried. Then I asked them to pray. I wish everybody in the whole world could have heard their prayer. Her dad decided he wanted to say the prayer to You, God. I know You forgave them and gave them the courage and strength to fulfill their promise to Courtney and to You. What a precious prayer he prayed to You, God. It was straight from his heart. We all four held hands and I thanked You, God, and asked You to bless their precious family. I prayed for the yelling and arguing to be a thing of the past. I know Your precious forgiveness came down from Heaven and enveloped them -- we could tell. We all stood up and hugged -- I was so professional, Lord -- I just cried and cried with them.

After they left I could have absolutely sprouted wings and gone clear up to Heaven. I was so excited! When something wonderful happens in my counseling session, I always go out and tell my secretary. She is so darling -- she has a fit right with me! We laugh and cry and thank God! Thank You for being so sweet and wonderful God. How precious You are. If all parents could look down like You do and see their little children . . . if they could only imagine what goes on in their precious little hearts . . . if they could only know what they're doing and how it affects their children, I know they would change. **May Your Holy Spirit work with each one of them.**

THE QUIET
Listener

Dear God,

This is such a wonderful time to sit down and talk to You. In a million years I'll never be able to thank You enough for letting me be a marriage and family counselor. For all these years I've had the privilege of trying to help people with their problems, or at least give them some options. Oh Lord, I'm so grateful to You, but I also know what a great responsibility it is. When people finally decide to talk to a counselor, they're usually ready to try out new ideas -- many are ready to try anything! That's a huge responsibility! Lord, I love what I'm doing! It's the most exciting thing in the world to see the hope that comes across some of their faces. We know that only You can change things and make them different. I always get tickled because once in a while I'm introduced as an expert. There aren't any experts -- those are just people that are away from home. I have to quickly let them know that I'm not an expert -- only Jesus Christ is the expert -- and I want to keep the line open between us.

If there is one thing I have learned, Lord, it's that the best counseling is listening. I will never forget, years ago, before I had ever done any professional counseling, Chuck and I were living in Midland and working with the young people from our church. When you work with young people, they're around quite a bit -- but we loved them. We had them morning, noon, and night, but we loved every minute of it. Our kiddos were young and they enjoyed the older ones coming by and seeing them. Then, I remember just like it happened yesterday, a young 15 year-old named Karen, called me crying. It was after school, and she said, "Mrs. Caldwell, would you please, please let me come talk to you." I said, "Of course you can come talk to me, darling." About 20 minutes later she came up the sidewalk, just crying her eyes out. She came and sat on the sofa by me and I said, "Honey, what's bothering you?" When she started talking, I couldn't have gotten a word in edgewise if I had wanted to. She just talked and talked for about an hour and a half. When she finally ran down, about all I had said was, "I'm sorry," and "Oh, that's too bad." She grabbed me around the neck and said, "Oh, Mrs. Caldwell, I could have never made it without you. Thank you, I appreciate you so much." And she ran out the front door. Well, I was kind of stunned. I sat there thinking, "What did I do to help? . . . How did I help her? I didn't even utter three words!"

Chuck saw her go out the front door as he came in and ask, "Was that Karen running down the street? What's wrong?" I said, "Oh, Chuck, I want to tell you about her," and I told him that she had asked to come over and talk. I told him that Karen had really needed to talk and that I never opened my mouth. He said, "Oh, Marge, that's wonderful! I wish you would counsel with me like that!" I thought, "I'm learning how to counsel by keeping my mouth shut."

In the first years, I learned that the best thing a counselor can do is to be very quiet and let the counselee get things off their chest. I learned to control my expressions, and to listen with my mind, but especially with my heart. I have really enjoyed counseling. I work with young people most of the time, so I've had quite a bit of experience in the area of high school and college, and it's awesome!

There is high school camp that I go to every summer with our church. We have a senior and junior high camp. The senior high camp is the one I usually go to because I teach college freshmen and I love getting to know them at camp. I do a lot of counseling at camp which helps me feel closer to the young people and helps me to know a little more about what's going on in their hearts and lives. I am so sad to think about some of the things they have to face, so much separation and divorce . . . heartache and arguing . . . name calling with their parents . . . and peer pressure! As I talk to them at camp, my heart goes out to them, because I know what a miserable life some of them are living. A teenager needs to be having fun and enjoying life. I have a friend who has a 14 year-old teenager. The other day during breakfast, her mother asked, "You seem so preoccupied, what's wrong?" The 14 year-old said, "Well, tomorrow is my birthday and I'll be 15 and we're not supposed to get along anymore. I love you and I know you love me. I want us to get along but somebody told me that when I got to be 15, I wouldn't get along with my parents anymore." I thought, what a joke! But what a wonderful teenager to really like her parents and appreciate their friendship.

I run into all kinds of kids at camp and all kinds of problems -- problems of rape, incest, and things you just can't believe. They try to cope with it by themselves, but it's hard. It is so exciting to me, to be able to tell them that Jesus Christ is real -- that You want to help them, and You are completely aware of the situation they are living in. One particular girl told me, "I can't get anybody to listen to me. My friends don't know what I'm talking about half the time. I know they care, but they don't understand because their home isn't like mine. I need someone to listen. I need to tell somebody what is going on in my home." So I sat down with her, and told her we had a long time. We sat on a bench under some trees and I listened while she poured her heart out. I don't know how long we sat there but it seemed like hours. It got dark and everyone else was called in for dinner. She and I just sat there. She talked and cried, and talked and cried, and I didn't open my mouth but to say "I'm sorry," and shake my head. That precious girl got so much off of her heart and out of her mind. She cried and said, "It's just so terrible to be full of anger and bitterness, and hate what's going on. I don't want to hate my mother and father, I know I'm supposed to love them, but I hate what's happening in my home." She was full of guilt. After she poured out her heart, we had prayer and she prayed first. I'll never forget what she said; it has influenced my counseling until this day. She said, "God, I want to thank You for sending somebody who wouldn't preach to me, but would just sit and listen. As I've talked God, I can see that some of the problem might be mine and I've got to pray more for my mother and daddy and quit being so critical of them. I need to realize how hard the things are that they deal with." I would like to take some credit for that wisdom, but I can't, because I hadn't opened my mouth.

God, it's really You that works in the heart. I want to thank You for letting me be the quiet listener.

ARE YOU LISTENING?

Dear God,

Aren't we funny creatures? But, You love us anyway. Sometimes we think that You only answer prayers with, "yes" or "no," but I feel like You have a few more ways to answer. Sometimes when we pray, and You answer immediately, like we wanted, we are so excited and feel very "spiritual." Other times, when You say "No," we throw a spiritual fit. We feel like our prayers got no higher than the ceiling. We complain that You don't hear our prayers, and we feel "unspiritual."

I have a friend from long ago who said to me, "Marge, look at my prayer library. I have every book on prayer that's been written, and I still can't seem to pray like I should." I told her, "You know there are books on how to pray, when to pray, when not to pray, and where to sit when you pray. But the complete work on prayer is found in God's Book. It's a little like swimming. You can read every book on how to swim, when to swim, where to swim, and what to wear, but you'll never know how to swim until you get in the water." Sometimes I get tickled when I hear someone pray in church in an unnatural tone of voice, using seven syllable words. I have a mental picture of You, looking down and saying, "Just get on with it."

Well, as I mentioned before, I believe there are more than just "yes and "no" answers to our prayers. You say, "yes," and we're thrilled. You say, "no," and we throw a fit. When You say "Wait awhile," that drives me up the wall, across the ceiling, and down the other side. Patience is not one of my virtues. Sometimes You might say, "I'm not going to give you what you asked for, I'm going to give you something better."

The best example I recall, of this particular answer to prayer, happened while we were living in Midland, Texas. Chuck was an area manager for his company and his goal was to become the sales manager. One day the sales manager retired and everyone thought Chuck would move to Houston and take his place. People phoned him from all over the country because they just knew he'd get the position. Of course, I was doubly excited because that would mean returning to Houston and "my roots." Chuck said we should pray everyday that "If it's right for us, we'll get it, but if it's not, for God to shut the door." It was easy for me to pray, "Thy will be done," because I knew it was going to happen.

One day Chuck called me and said he didn't get the position. I was as much help to him as Job's wife. I cried and cried and had a major pity-party. To add insult to injury, the company sent the new sales manager out for Chuck to train. That was the last straw. For a few weeks, we acted like there had been a death in the family. One night Chuck sat me down for a talk. "Marge, didn't we pray and say we'd accept God's will? Now we have to work hard and keep trusting Him." I said, "But it was easy to pray for God's will when I thought it was what I wanted."

A few months passed and one day Chuck called home, "Get packed! We're moving to Houston. I have a new job as the Vice President of Marketing." I was astounded. That was the job over the job we'd prayed for. I want to tell You, God, we felt like spiritual spoiled brats when we asked You to forgive us. Thank You for being such an understanding God and knowing the frailty of our humanness.

I am reminded of Your precious promise in Jeremiah 29:11, "I know the plans I have for you, declares the Lord, plans to prosper you and not to harm you, plans to give you a hope and a future." How true. **Thank You, Lord.**

LESSONS
ON Joy

Dear God,

I'm so happy! I'm as happy as a "bug in a rug!" While I'm saying this, I realize I have a lot of sayings that are strange. For instance, "You look like Miss Astor," and "Drunk as a sailor," and "Birds of a feather flock together." My little brother and I would "roll in the aisle" (there it is again) with laughter because Mother would roll her eyes and say, "A stitch in time is worth two in the bush," or "A bird in the hand gathers no moss." She could never understand why we got so tickled.

I used to think happiness and joy were the same thing. And then I learned that happiness depends on things, or people, or situations. Joy is a gift from You, God. I think of my mother (my father was a violent alcoholic); she loved You so much. After a terrible night, as long as I can remember, Mother would wake me up with a glass of juice and say, "Good morning, darlin'. Oh, I wonder what God is going to do for us today? Wonder what we can do for Him?" When I was old enough to understand the situation, I would say, "How can you do this, Mother?" She would answer, "Just Jesus, darlin' -- just Jesus!" That must have warmed Your heart, dear God.

One time my husband and I were vacationing in Colorado and we found a beautiful little stream near our cabin. The water was splashing in the sun, over the rocks, and out of its banks, but quickly got back to splashing again. Then, as it progressed downstream, we noticed that the water became calmer! That was because it was deeper. Same rocks, same water, same direction -- but smoother. So much like our relationship with You, God. If our faith is shallow, like that little stream in Colorado, we'll be full of anxiety, fearful, worried, and afraid. Our faith will be weak . . . strong . . . and then weak again. But as we deepen our relationship with You, we have the same rocks and the same direction, but there is peace and joy that makes our life smoother and calmer. **Same problems, same situation, but an over-riding, unexplainable peace. Thank You, God. Philippians 4:6-7.**

I'M BURNED Out

Dear God,

I want to talk to You today about my life and serving You. I'm burned out, Lord. I feel unsettled and anxious. I don't know which way to turn. I've been in so many activities at church for all these years. Somehow I believed that everytime I was offered an opportunity to serve, then You were asking me. I always felt like I had to take it because I wanted to follow Your will and please You. It took me a while to realize that everything that's offered isn't necessarily what You want me to do. It may be an affirmation, or it may not. I got really involved and then took a step back for a while, but now I'm right back in the middle of everything. I'm running my legs off trying to do what I think You want me to do, yet I know there's something wrong with this. If we're serving You, we're supposed to enjoy what we're doing. We're not supposed to let it wear us down. We should have peace when we're serving You. I feel like my mind and body are going 90 miles an hour and I just can't settle down. I know there is something wrong, but I can't seem to figure it out.

I went to a meeting this morning and it was the funniest thing. I didn't really want to go, but I felt like I should because it had to do with the Bible study I'm teaching. As I sat there and listened, I thought, "Why Lord, You didn't send me here to learn what to teach. You sent me here to learn what I need to quit doing." It came to me while I was sitting in the meeting, "Why am I serving You like I am? I'm frustrated and frantically going from one activity to the other. I hardly have time to turn around or to breathe because I'm so busy getting things tended to. Why am I doing all this? Am I serving You because I want to, or am I doing it for some other reason?" All these questions lead back to my frustration and my tiredness. I'm physically, emotionally, and spiritually tired. I know You don't want your children to be spiritually tired, emotionally drained, or physically worn out, because it's not a good testimony.

While I was in the meeting, I began to mull over what I was doing. I asked myself, "Am I doing all these things because You want me to do, because I want to, or because I like the attention I get?" Sitting there, I began to feel so ashamed of what was going through my mind. All of a sudden the teacher said, "I want you all to turn to Psalm 46 and look at the tenth verse." Lord, I nearly died! My mind had been racing, trying to figure out what on earth I was supposed to be doing and what was next on my agenda. I read Psalm 46:10, and I couldn't believe it. It said "Be still and know that I am God. I will be exalted among the nations, I will be exalted in the earth." Those words really hit me -- "Be still and know that I am God."

I got to thinking about that and I don't think I heard another word the teacher said. When it was over I said good-bye to everyone, went out to my car, and came home. I've been sitting here thinking about what that scripture says. "Be still and know that I am God." I figure the only way to know more about You is to be still. I'm never still, Lord! Even when I'm sitting down, doing nothing, I'm thinking about what I ought to be doing, or feeling guilty because I'm not up doing something that I really should be doing. I never give my spirit time to be still and to realize that Your kingdom is going to get along great without me! What happens in Your kingdom doesn't depend a bit on what I do or don't do. I began to think about the exalted idea I have of myself and my importance in Your kingdom. God, I know You love me and I know You want me to serve You, and I want to serve You. What it all boils down to is, I'm suffering from a little burn-out. It's taken the joy out of my service to You, and that's wrong! I know You want us to enjoy what we're doing for You, so we can be a perfectly wonderful testimony to somebody else.

The other day someone stopped me in the hall at church and asked me to pray for them. I thought, "Oh I better not forget that." I was afraid I'd get busy and forget it. It's such a compliment to me, Lord, when someone asks me to pray for them. We should never be too busy to do that. Lord, help me to never be so busy that I might forget to pray for someone who asks me to.

I'm glad I went to that meeting. I don't think I learned much about the lesson except for Psalm 46:10, but I got one thing out of it -- I have to apply that scripture to my life! I'm going to choose time to be still and realize all over again that You are the Master. You are in charge of everything, including me and my service to You. If I allow it, You will be in charge of everything I do. I'm so busy running around in circles, I don't even stand still long enough to find the "peace that passes all understanding" -- to be still and know that You are God. Without doing anything objectionable to Your Word, I want to paraphrase that a little bit -- I want to be still and get to know You better, Lord. That's what I want, I want to know You better. If I'm going to know You better, I've got to have time to study and read about You, then You will teach me how to be still.

Lord, I'm excited! I went to the meeting frustrated because I had so much to do. I left the meeting (I don't even remember what it was about) and all I remember is that scripture, Psalm 46:10. I know You spoke to me this morning. You want me to be still and get to know You better. Lord, I think I'll start evaluating what I'm doing and try to prioritize. Help me to clearly see what You've called me to, and what You haven't. I want to spend more time with You.

Lord, what a deal! I got all dressed up today to go and learn how to do something, and You taught me how to let go of some of it. Whatever You want me to let go of, God, whatever You want me to do, Lord, that's what I want to do. There's one thing I know already -- You don't want me to be burned out by trying to do so much. Whatever my motives are in serving You, if I take on too much, then I may be a poor testimony for someone else. I may keep them from serving if they see that I'm dog-tired all the time. I've learned a lesson today, Lord, and I thank You for it. Help me to remember that when I am still, I get to know You better. I want to be still and let Your precious Holy Spirit speak to me. Thank You for Psalm 46:10. I've known that scripture for years, but it's never spoken to me like it did today in the meeting. The way You speak to us is exciting, so sweetly, and so softly, if we'll just be still and listen. **Thank You, I've learned a very valuable lesson today. I love You, Lord.**

WHO'S SPEAKING to Me, God or Satan?

Dear God,

For many years I would ask You over and over, "Are You talking to me, or is it Satan?" I was so confused. I wanted to do what You wanted me to do, but I was afraid Satan might sneak in, and I'd do something I shouldn't.

I will never forget that day when I was flying home from Atlanta. I had that little tray down, my Bible open, and I was trying to find concepts and principles in Your Word. Concepts and principles are teachings from scripture that tell us what You want, but let us choose what we will do. I'm thinking of Matthew 6:33 where You tell us to seek You and all these things will be added.

As I looked out of the window, I began asking You how to know Your voice instead of Satan's. All of a sudden I heard you say, "Marge." Well, I wondered what on earth was going on. If You had spoken to me audibly, I'd have been so scared, I'd have jumped out of the plane. There was no audible voice -- but just as clear and bright as a neon sign, I heard in my mind, "Satan always comes in questions, and I come in statements!" Aren't we funny creatures? I still wondered if You were speaking to me. When we're confused, the best thing to do is lay that problem beside Your Word. If it fits, accept it. If it contradicts Your Word, then trash it.

So I started with Eve. How did Satan come to her? "Can you eat of everything in the Garden?" Eve answered. "Yes, everything but that tree over there. God said don't touch it." Satan asked, "Why not? Because He doesn't want you to be as smart as He is?" God, You must have been hurt when Adam and Eve disobeyed you. There it was -- a question!

Then I went to Job. Everybody needs friends like Job had. They asked Job, "What have you done? You must have done something wrong because God is punishing you." And his wife, what an inspiration she was, "Why don't you just curse God and die?" A question again.

And You, our precious Savior, in the wilderness while being tempted, You heard the questions, "Are you hungry? Why don't you change these stones into bread?" You answered Satan as only You would. Then Your Word says Satan took You to the pinnacle and said, "If You're the Son of God, bow down and worship me and I'll give you the world." It thrills me, God, to read how You quoted scripture to him, even while he had the audacity to tempt You and misquote You.

Then I remembered Peter and how he denied that he knew You when a little servant girl asked him. Questions again.

Now, I think about how Satan comes to me, "Don't you think you should stop running around like this? Don't you think you're too old to be teaching young people? Why don't you take a sabbatical leave and have fun with your friends?" When I was having an especially hard battle with the devil, God, you always came through to solve it. I walked out to get the mail one day, and saw a letter from someone I didn't know. I won't quote it verbatim, but she kept saying, "Don't stop going to schools and talking to the students. Five years ago I was a high school senior, getting ready to make the mistake of my life. When you came to speak, I didn't plan to listen, but you kept us laughing, and I wanted to hear more. Your talk changed the course of my life! I will always be grateful to you." She underlined a P.S., "Don't stop going to young people!" God, You knew I would need encouragement that day, and the note had been written two days earlier! You are never five minutes early or five minutes late. You are just on time! Thank You, God.

Thank You for coming to us in statements: Matthew 6:33, Psalm 37:4, 1 Peter 3:15, and on and on. Now, I don't have as much trouble discerning your Word. If it's a question to me, then I know it's really a temptation from you-know-who! But if I know Your Word, then I can remind myself of Your statements of love, care, and mercy. I think of James 4:7. That's very plain, and I thank You for it.
Goodnight, God. I'll see you in the morning. I love You, God.

A CHANGED Life

Dear God,

I'm thrilled about what happens when someone truly finds You as their Savior. It's so exciting to play a little part in their life and be there when it happens. I'm just beside myself tonight because I keep thinking about the wonderful thing that happened at the counseling center. Lord, You know how many times I've wanted to see You act quickly, but I have rarely seen a time as dramatic as this. You remember your precious child, Jody, before she gave her heart to you? She came to see me when she was very sad because her husband had left her with four children.

It's so amazing how she found her way into our counseling center! She had been under mountains of stress and a friend told her that what she needed was a good massage! The massage therapist told Jody that her shoulders and arms were very tight and asked her what was wrong. Jody told her about her husband leaving and said that she didn't know which way to turn. She felt sad and defeated. The therapist said, "Oh, I know where you can get some help! Why don't you go down to The First Baptist Church Counseling Center? They will have someone who can help you." God, it's amazing to me how You get people into the places You want them! And You use so many of us to help You do it. It frightens me that You might want to use me in a particular way, but I have been too stubborn or too busy to know.

Nevertheless, Jody came to our counseling center, and oh, dear God, the first time she walked into my room! She looked like a basket-case and I thought, "Poor thing, she is really having a hard time." Well, we introduced ourselves and she told me about her situation. She talked about the difficult divorce trial that was ahead.

She was so afraid of the hard times that were sure to come. After our hour was up, I said, "Jody, when I finish counseling I always ask the Lord to help us know which way to turn, because none of us knows the answer to everything." She sat straight up, her eyes burned with anger, and she said, "I'm Jewish." I said, "Oh, that's fabulous! I'm so excited that you're the real thing!" I told her that I loved the Jews and that Jesus was a Jew. I asked her again if I could pray for her. She didn't say anything, so I prayed. When Jody left, the look on her face made me think that I'd never see her again. Oh, I wanted her to come back so I could tell her more about Jesus.

The next week I nearly died when I looked at the appointment book, and her name was on my schedule! I could hardly wait! When she came back we talked more about her situation -- what we could do and the best way for her to go. At the end of our session, I said, "Now, Jody, you know that I always pray." She said, "Yes, I know." I held her hand and I prayed to You, God, and oh, how I felt Your presence in the room! I felt like someway, somehow, You were really working on this young woman. Dear God, I want to thank You for letting me see You work and allowing me to be a part of something so wonderful! Jody left that day and I prayed I would see her again.

The third time she came in I was thrilled! When she sat down I asked her what happened that week. She looked at me and said she didn't want to talk about that. God, my heart nearly stopped! I asked her what she wanted to talk about. Jody said, "I want to know why you think Jesus is so real?" I laughed and said, "Now Jody, that's like saying, sic'em to a dog, because I would really love to tell you why I think Jesus is so real." And, oh dear God, thank You, thank You, thank You for putting the words in my mouth to tell her why You are real and why You are the Messiah. Jody and I had prayer before she left.

About ten days later she walked into the counseling center and said she didn't want to talk about her situation. Instead, she wanted to know a little bit more about Jesus. God, was Your heart so happy that day? It must have been! I told her more about You. I quoted Isaiah and showed her in Your word how the Jews could find You if they would only read the Old Testament. At the end of the hour, she said, "I want to pray and ask Jesus Christ to come into my heart." I'm so glad you are a God of Your word. I'm so glad that when we tell someone about You, You keep the promise from Matthew 7, "if they seek, they will find." This precious Jewish lady had been devastated, but found new strength and wonderment in You.

God, I never realized what a sense of guilt some people have, especially Jewish people, when they accept You as Savior. You see, she was very active in her synagogue and that meant her four children would be affected. She couldn't tell anyone about her salvation because it might affect her custody battle. So, as the days passed, I saw firsthand how hard life can become when someone has asked You into their heart.

Most of Jody's family lived in the Midwest and she didn't dare tell any of them what had happened because she knew it would break their hearts. She didn't know what they would do. She couldn't even tell her four children. So, she began her new life by coming to our church every Sunday and Wednesday night. She grew like a weed! I have never seen anything like it! When she went to nurse's training at Houston Baptist University, I saw your hand in her life every time we turned around. It was exciting to see how You sent people to her, sending her to different places to get help, and helping her to grow and absorb the Bible! Oh Lord, it must have thrilled Your heart like it thrilled mine. She continually read the Bible, took good courses at HBU, and began to grow. She couldn't say too much about it, and she couldn't read her Bible at home. When her mother and father visited her from out-of-state, she had to hide everything that even resembled Christianity because they would have been outraged. She didn't want anyone to know until it was the right time. Of course, she was so excited she wanted to tell everyone right away, but she couldn't! One night, Lord, I never will forget. You must have gotten a real bang out of it too! The phone rang about two o'clock in the morning, and Jody said, "Oh Marge, it's all in Isaiah!" And I said, "What?" She said, "Oh, every bit of it's in Isaiah -- the Jews can find Jesus as their Savior if they'll just read their own books!" I said, "I know, I know." Oh, she was so excited, and I was too. Lord, I want to thank You for letting me be a part of that.

Well that was five years ago. What has happened in the meantime thrills my heart. I have never seen anybody grow like Jody. When she graduated from Houston Baptist University and became a nurse -- Cum Laude -- I nearly burst with pride. I know you looked down at that precious young lady, who had been so miserable and so down-hearted, with pride. She has found such joy and courage in You. Isn't it wonderful that her youngest son has accepted You and her two oldest children are seeking You? She told all of her family and they were amazed, yet saddened. Because they have seen such a change in her, they are now wondering if there isn't something to this Jesus thing. Oh Lord, thank You! When we can see a life change, when we see how You change a person, it's the greatest thing on earth. The only thing that can change our world is to change people from the inside out.

As I talk to You this morning, Lord, I think of Jody and how her life has changed. She is full of joy about You. I think about the suffering and persecution she endured when she accepted You as her Savior. Most of us live sheltered lives. We don't know the heartache people from other cultures and religions face when they ask You into their hearts. I don't believe there is anything more beautiful than a brand new Christian who is really excited about what You are doing in their life. As I look at Jody now, I know you have your hand on her life. She is a nurse at M.D. Anderson Cancer Center here in Houston. I see how You take a person who feels like their life isn't worth living, and lift them up. Everything seemed to pile in on Jody when she was in the pit, but I saw you pull her out and put her feet on solid ground. You straightened her life out and gave her joy, peace, and encouragement.

Oh Lord, it's so wonderful . . . I wish everybody could be there when a life is changed. Then people would catch the vision of what it's like to be born again. It's not a new life piled on top of the old one. It's old things having passed away, and behold, everything becomes new. Second Corinthians 5:17 is the scripture that I think of. Old things pass away when we accept you as Savior, and everything becomes new again. Oh, it's wonderful. Thank You for the experiences of this life that enhance our faith and help us feel closer to You. We know You live in our hearts if we've asked You to. We know You're interested in every little thing and I saw that lived out for me in Jody. **Thank you, Lord, for changing lives.**

GOD'S SENSE of HUMOR

Dear God,

What a sense of humor You must have! When You glance down at your creation and see the crazy things we do -- You must get tickled to death. I was thinking about the other day when I overbooked. I planned to be at two houses at noon to do a program. Being at two places at the same time is impossible, but I didn't want to admit my mistake -- so I just tried to act like I knew what I was doing.

I went to the first house (a very large, beautiful house) and a lady answered the door. Beyond her, I could see a lot of ladies sitting around eating lunch. So I said, "Good afternoon. I'm Marge Caldwell, and I've come to entertain you!" She said, "Come in." I walked back to the den and started my program. They laughed in the right places and seemed to enjoy it. When I finished I thanked them and the hostess took me to the door. I said I'd enjoyed being there and told her she could send my check to my home or office. She looked shocked, then said, "I've never seen you or talked to you in my life!" I asked, "Aren't you Mrs. So and So?" She said, "No, her party is down the block."

Well, I'll have you know that I gave three party entertainments that day. Running from house to house, I began to see just exactly how I could have avoided all the confusion. I could have spent a few minutes on the phone explaining my dilemma and making arrangements suitable to everyone. But no, I had to act like Mrs. Superwoman and try to cover up my mistake.

Isn't that the way we do so many times in our spiritual lives? We make a bad mistake and spend time rationalizing. We think things like, "It wasn't my fault," or "If I had been the chairperson it would have never come to this," or "I knew it wouldn't work." We rationalize our mistakes, then say "God knew that was too much for me." Sometimes one little phone call would settle everything. One statement like, "I'm sorry it happened, but we can fix it easily," can solve so much. How we rationalize with you, Lord. I've even said that if I'm given long enough -- I can make anything I've done look like it's Chuck's fault!

If I would only call out to You, Lord. Just a little prayer of "help" real quickly, and You can solve the whole thing in a matter of minutes. Sometimes we need to come to You and confess. That's hard for most of us. It involves a little thing called pride. We don't want to admit a mistake . . . we'd prefer to pass the buck.

But You, dear God, in Your infinite grace and mercy, look down on us and smile. I can hear You say, "You're forgiven. Now take the blame if it's yours. I'll help you pick up the pieces and get going." Lord, **You created us, and You must really enjoy us sometimes. Thank You for loving us.**
1 John 1:9.

FEELING &
Doing are Worlds Apart

Dear God,

Thank you for every little detail of my life. Some days it's harder to thank You than others. Some days I wake up and love everybody, and then other days I wake up and my back hurts or I have a headache and my body feels out of sync. I don't like anybody or anything in those moments. I just feel blah! But God, I've learned at that time to sit down in my "devotion time" chair and read the Bible (even though I don't want to), and tell You how I feel. I might as well, You know it anyway.

I'm so glad you keep Your word and don't zap us to make us do what You want. I know that having the power of choice is part of being made in Your image. Every now and then I wish You'd write what You want us to know on the wall, so we could be certain about what You're saying. Then I remember that in the Old Testament You did just that, and it wasn't a good message! So I don't wish that anymore.

As I sit here reading Your Word, I begin to realize again how awesome You really are. Something begins to happen. My bad attitude softens some, and Your Word can get through to me. Before I realize it, I'm asking You to forgive my arrogance and make me a blessing to someone that day.

Wow! Lord, how excited I get when I realize that You understand these mood swings! One thing I've learned -- I don't feel my way into doing -- I do my way into feeling! So whether I like it or not, I must do it, and the feeling follows. Thank You, God. I think of Galatians 2:20. That seems to fit for this day. **I love You, my dear Savior.**

DEAR GOD

LIFE IS FUNNy

Dear God,

Sometimes I find myself doing the funniest things, and most of the time they are connected with airports or airplanes. One morning really early, I was on the way to the airport. I was praying, "Oh God, don't let there be an accident in front of me." What a selfish prayer. I was very late and by the time I parked the car, checked my luggage, and went through security, I was really late. As I hurried to the gate I saw that horrible sign, "Now Boarding." I ran out to the plane and a man was just closing the door. I screamed, "Oh I've got to get on this plane! I've got to get on this plane!" He said, "Okay lady, I'll open the door." So he knocked on the door and they opened it. I jumped in. I was breathing so hard I thought I was going to faint. I took the first available seat. The next thing I knew, the flight attendant got up and began to say all of those psychologically unsound things . . . like if that yellow thing falls down, what you're supposed to do. I don't listen to her, because if that little yellow thing falls down, I will die of fright right there.

The lady next to me asked me what I did and where I lived, all the things passengers ask each other. The plane started taxiing out and she said, "Where are you going?" I said, "Midland, Texas." She said, "Not on this plane." I screamed, "Where is this plane going?" "Greenville, SC." I jumped up. Have you ever jumped up with your seatbelt fastened? My tummy wasn't the same for days. I ran to the flight attendant and screamed, "I've got to get off this plane." She said, "So you're the one. I've been talking for five minutes about someone who is on this plane who doesn't belong here." I said, "Please let me off." I was about to cry. Her face was smiling but her eyes were glaring at me. She went up to the pilot's door and knocked while I stood in the aisle. Perfectly wonderful people can be so ugly. They glared at me and I kept saying, "I'm sorry." In a few minutes the plane taxied back to the airport. Then the glares turned to real hostility. When we got to the gate, the same man who let me on was standing there. As I passed him I said, "Oh, I had a wonderful trip." I will never forget the look on his face.

As I am sitting here thinking about that trip, I think about our spiritual lives. We are so busy trying to do Your work that we neglect, or don't care to read, the warning signs. You tell us many times, "You're on the wrong road," but we like the highway we're on, and don't want to take the road You have chosen. Thank You for always being there to guide me back when I decide to return. What a wonderful God You are. I can just hear You saying, "Marge, there were three signs right in front of you saying South Carolina. You didn't pay attention because you thought you knew how to go without me." I want to thank You for that God. It reminds me of Proverbs 3:5-6, **"Trust in the Lord with all your heart and lean not on your own understanding; in all your ways acknowledge Him, and He will make your paths straight."**

SHE CAN'T COOK
or Sew, But She Makes Me Happy

Dear God,

I am sitting here reminiscing this morning and having a lovely time with You. I just want to thank You again for my husband. When I see some of the things that husbands do to their families these days, I am very glad to have been married all these years to a man who has helped me be the best person I can be. We've had a wonderful life together, but as I sit here thinking about myself as a bride, I nearly turn green thinking about all the mistakes I've made, all the things I didn't do, and then all the things I did, do but wished I hadn't.

I've always lived in a big city and had never been to a farm until I met Chuck at college. Chuck was from a farm way out in West Texas. He had two older brothers and two younger brothers and he was in the middle. I am so thankful for the many, many things his mother taught him, especially how to be sensitive to other people's needs. Ever since I've known him, he has been sensitive to women's needs. I didn't appreciate that as much in the beginning of our marriage but I grew to appreciate it later.

Chuck and I were getting serious and talking about marriage, so my mother and I went out to the farm to meet his family. I had never been on a farm and when I whistled at the chickens -- his family nearly died! I didn't know what you did with chickens except eat them! Chuck's father took me out to watch the cows being milked and I was so embarrassed -- the closest I had ever been to a cow was driving by a pasture. The farm was kind of scary to me because I didn't know what to do about anything. Chuck's family got a big bang out of me and teased me for years.

Chuck was the first of the five boys to get married. After a few years two of the other brothers married girls that had grown up on neighboring farms. Those girls understood all about cooking and sewing -- the only time I had ever sewn anything was when I was senior in high school and took home economics. I tried to make a blouse but I put the sleeves in backwards and of course didn't make a good grade. I felt like I was a failure! Not only could I not sew, but I didn't know a whole lot about cooking either. I could boil water and make good sandwiches, but I didn't do too much else! I tried to learn. I never learned to cook growing up because a lady had been with us for years who did all the cooking.

So, we went out to meet Chuck's family and they got a big kick out of me trying to adjust to the farm. Right after we got there, I asked Chuck's little sister where the bathroom was because I hadn't seen one around. She said, "Oh, you just walk out the back door and down the path" and she pointed the way. I was a little nervous and tried to clarify, "Ruth, is that the bathroom?" She said, "Yes." I asked her, "What happens if you have to go at night?" She said, "We've made arrangements for that," and she showed me a little pot that was placed by the bed. Well, I was pretty uncomfortable about it all and felt unsure of myself. Then I wondered where they bathed, and Ruth educated me about that too.

After Chuck and I had been married a short while, we went out to visit. I called Chuck's mother, Mother Bess. One afternoon we were all sitting around the dining table and Chuck was sitting directly across the table from me. There was always a crowd at their table because they had such a large family, including the grandparents. Mother Bess was talking to the two daughter-in-laws and they were talking about wonderful recipes they had tried out. Oh, they just sounded so good! All three of them were exchanging recipes with one another. Then Mother Bess talked to the two girls about a dress she was making. They were talking about recipes and dress patterns, and I felt like a dummy! I thought I don't know anything about sewing and I don't know much about cooking -- I felt like a failure. I guess the expression on my face was showing a little bit because Chuck did the most wonderful, sensitive thing that day in the dining room. He got up and walked around the table and put his hands on my shoulders and said, "You know, Marge can't cook or sew, but I tell you, she makes me happy and that just thrills me to death." Then he turned around and walked back to his seat. I felt ten feet tall! Those two sister-in-laws would rather have that said about them than all the cooking and sewing in the whole world. I sat up straight and felt so good. Chuck's mother looked over at me with great admiration and said, "That was a precious thing to do, Chuck, and I'm so glad that she makes you happy. That's the most important thing in the world." So, I decided that day that making my husband happy was a lot more important than cooking and sewing.

Not long ago Chuck talked to a big group at our church, and he made this remark, "Well, Marge can't cook or sew, but she makes me happy," and he looked over me and grinned. Then he said, "You know if I want to hide anything from Marge, I just put it in the oven." Now, that was tacky and uncalled for. Of course they all laughed and I didn't really care -- it was funny! I don't mind not being a gourmet cook. I used to worry because I didn't want Chuck to be disappointed in me, but I'm not worried anymore because I know it takes more than a delicious meal or the ability to sew to make a man happy. Now, I'm not putting down either one of those things. Every once in a while I wish I could cook something that was served at a friend's dinner party; or when I see someone make a beautiful jacket or dress, I think, "Oh, I wish I had learned how to do that." But those feelings don't stay long, because the most important thing I've learned is how to make my husband happy.

Thank You, God, that I don't beat myself up anymore over the things I never learned how to do. Thank You for what I can do, and the special gifts You've given me as Chuck's wife. **I'm so excited because all these years, Chuck has told me over and over, how much it meant to him that I made him feel important. I'm so thrilled over that. Thank You, Lord.**

TIRED Mother

Dear God,

This morning I feel fat, sloppy, and ugly -- almost like a monster. I feel awful. I don't know exactly why, except my attitude is really showing. You know, God, I get tired of changing diapers, cleaning up drool, fixing formula, and getting up half the night with the babies crying. I never thought in all my born days that I would have twins -- twins! And I have a four year-old too! Lord it's just so much. Bill and I had no idea that we would be blessed with so many kids all at one time. And to think, we were afraid we couldn't even have one. God, I love my babies, and I love Bill, but I feel so untidy. It seems like I'm always wearing this old housecoat -- it's so comfortable it feels like my brother. I know Bill must be tired of looking at it.

When I think of Bill, I am envious of how he goes out in the world everyday. He gets to talk to real people, and carry on normal conversations with grown-ups. I think I've forgotten how to carry on a conversation with anybody! I think about it God and I'm just so tired. Besides that, I'm the only woman in our neighborhood who doesn't have a career. They all get dressed and go to work everyday. I stay home and work, but a lot of people don't really consider it work. When we have neighborhood parties, all the women look so sharp and wear all the latest styles, their hair is perfect, and their nails are manicured. My nails look like I've chewed them off to my first knuckle, in fact, I think I have. Lord, You didn't give me hair when I passed by You -- You gave me chicken feathers, it always needs to be combed or curled, or something. I just feel tacky, that's all.

When Bill and I take his clients and their wives out to dinner, I try so hard to look sharp, because I want him to be proud of me! But then one of the wives will say, in a sweet voice no less, "And tell me about you." About that time I start feeling like I just want to throw up. Does she really want to hear about me? My life consists of baby twins, and a four year-old. Does she want to hear about how I can hardly get anything done around the house between changing diapers and fixing formula? Does she want to hear about how little sleep I get (even though Bill helps with the babies) or my nightmares about running out of formula! I wonder how interested she would be to hear what my house is like most of the time, and what it's like to take care of two little bitty babies at the same time -- one screaming and one sleeping, waking each other up, and all that stuff! I wonder if I told her that, what would happen?

Actually, God, do you remember one night when I did? I thought, well, this sharp-looking lady wants to know what I do, so I'll just tell her. I told her from beginning to end what I did nearly every day, and added a few little errands like going to the grocery store and the dry cleaners. You should've seen her face -- it was so funny, I got tickled myself! She looked shocked! She said, "How do you do all that?" I said to myself, "I don't know, I must be superwoman and don't even know it." After I finished the long tirade of what my day was like, I asked her what she did. She said, "Oh, it's sort of a dull job, I work for an insurance company. It's not a very interesting and my boss is a terror. My stomach is in knots everyday when I go to work and I usually come home with a headache. Sometimes I take it out on my husband. But you know, I wanted a career, and I went all out to get one. We decided if I was going to have a career that we would wait to have children. But as I've listened to you talk about your life and your children, it seems like what you do is far more important than what I do. I'm envious of you." Then she turned to her husband and said, "I want you to take a good look at this lady. She and her husband have twins that are three months old, plus a four year-old! She looks like she stepped out of Vogue!" And then she told her husband, "It makes me want to start having kids!"

I felt so funny, Lord, because I remember that when I was in college, I wanted to have career in fashion. All through college I modeled for a store here in town and they told me I was quite good. I loved it so much I decided to major in fashion-merchandising in college. I met my precious husband, then graduated with honors, and somehow my career took second place to the love I felt for him. He is such a smart man and has a great job. He told me that I didn't have to work after we were married because we could make it on his salary. I thought to myself, well, I want a career and I'll just start working anyway. We had long talks about how many kids we wanted, what they would be like, and how much we wanted to start our family while we were still young and could enjoy them. I thought I would work for a year or two and hadn't planned on having our four year-old as soon as we did. But, God, it seems like You had another plan for us! As I talk to You this morning, Lord, I remember what that lady said to me that night and how her husband said, "Bill, you've got a real looker here." I know You saw Bill beam from ear to ear, and he reached over and put his arms around me and said, "I do feel blessed. I am fortunate to have such a wonderful wife and mother to our kids."

As I think about that God, I realize that I could have thrown away the career of raising my children for a career in fashion-merchandising. My soul! There is no comparison! When the children are older, there will be plenty of time for a career. You know what, Lord, I'm so glad that I'm a mommy! When I started talking to You I felt sloppy and ugly. Now I don't feel that way. Thank You, Lord, for Your precious Holy Spirit that helps me when I talk things out with You. When I sit down, and pour my heart out, everything seems to fall into place. I am so proud of my family -- I love my children, I love my husband, and he loves me and the kids so much. We have a comfortable home, a happy home, and the three precious (and demanding) children. From now on, I'm going to hold my head high when I walk into a room with other ladies who have come from their offices and important jobs. I have just come from my career too, and I'm so proud to have the job of being a mother. I get to train my kids. I get to stay home and watch my children grow and change. I want to thank You for that Lord. Forgive me for the way I started out talking to You. I know my hair needs combing and I need to put on some makeup -- but I don't feel sloppy or ugly. I don't feel anything but excited because I am a mommy who is staying home with my kids. I remember something else Lord -- Proverbs 22:6 says, "Train a child in the way he should go, and when he is old he will not turn from it." That's what I'm doing, and it's a very important job! I'm "training up" three fabulous kiddos, so that if they do get off the beaten path when they're older, they'll have You to come back to. Thank You Lord. **I feel like superwoman right now!**

OFFICE Missionary

Dear God,

So many times I have wondered, "Why in the world did you put me in this job?" I know You sent me here to ask for a job. Even though I needed a job badly, I didn't really want it. I felt like You led me here and they hired me. I was excited about having a job, but I never dreamed what I was getting myself into. I never will forget the very first day. I felt confident that I could do the work, but I wasn't ready for all the stuff that was going on in the office. My co-workers took your name in vain, talked about You something awful, and told some of the filthiest jokes I have ever heard! When one of the men came over and told me a terrible joke, I was so surprised, I didn't know how to react. I've always worked in the church where you never hear bad language and everyone tries to be sweet to each other. I didn't have any idea what this secular job would be like. I tell You, Lord, I was really upset for a while, and blamed You for sending me. My whole Sunday School class had prayed that I would find the right job, and when I was hired, I went back and thanked the class for praying. Because of our prayers, I knew I was in the right job and that You had sent me!

For days I was in shock about all the stuff that went on in the office. They were always talking about what bar they were going to after work. After I had been there a while I saw other things going on that I knew were not Christian. In fact, Lord, after about six months, I found out that I was the only Christian in that office. I remember when I discovered that . . . I thought there had been a mistake somewhere . . . "I'm not supposed to be here," I thought. So the days went on and I was confident about my work performance. But everyone looked at me like I was crazy when I started reading my Bible during the morning and afternoon breaks. I would sit down and read Your word, asking for the strength and courage to deal with my co-workers. One day I suggested that we have a little Bible study at noon and asked if anyone was interested. They laughed! They looked at me like I was out to lunch, so I dropped the idea . . . for a while at least.

Then, God, they started calling me "Ms. Goody Two Shoes," and that really hurt me for a long time. I knew they didn't mean it as a compliment and I felt like I didn't have a friend among them. They were polite to me, and nice, but they walked around me like I had the plague or something. But one day, something happened that changed the whole tide of all the feelings in the office. One of the girls there was in a terrible accident and she was killed. Everyone in the office loved this girl, and I liked her too. Different ones began to come and sit at my desk and talk to me about her. Some of the girls would cry and I noticed they always came over to me.

After that, there was a day that was sort of the breakthrough. One of the ladies said, "I'm having trouble with one my teenage boys, and I wonder if you'd pray for me and for him." Oh, God, do You remember how excited I was! I told You all about it, and I began to see that maybe there was a reason for my being in that office. I told her, of course I would pray for her and her son. More than that, I told her I would do anything I could to help her. I worked with teenagers at my church and if there was anything I could do, I would be glad to. She looked at me and said, "You work with teenagers at your church?" And I said, "Yes, and oh, they're darling! They come over to the house quite often. They swim and I fix hot dogs or burgers. Do you think your son could come over?" She didn't think he would come and said that he would probably be rude to me if I invited him. She was so touched that I had even thought to include him. God, I never will forget how You turned everything around. Things began to be different.

He did come to the party. I told our youth group about

him and asked them to be really sweet to him and make him feel like he was a part of the group. He was a good swimmer -- better than most of the guys! And he was such a cute looking guy -- all of the girls thought he was darling! I think he ate more hot dogs than the rest of the guys put together, but he had a wonderful time. I was so proud of my teenage friends who were sweet to him and made him feel welcome.

God, I never will forget how You used that party to get him into our Sunday school class, where he began to learn about Jesus. At first he felt shy because he didn't know anything about anything, and the rest of the kids seemed to know so much. I watched him as he began to read his Bible. He was never absent from Sunday School and he was always there on time. One Sunday morning after class, I never will forget this God, he came up to me and thanked me for helping him. Then he said, "But I know I need Jesus Christ in my heart. Could you tell me how to do that?" Oh God, I had the privilege of helping him find You as his Savior and telling him all about You! He said he didn't know how to pray and I said, "That's all right, you just simply ask Jesus Christ to forgive you of your sins and come into your life." He prayed that morning to receive Jesus.

He began to change and then his mother began to change. She would thank me and talk about what a completely different kid he was. This sweet teenager kept working on his Mom, and eventually she came with him to church. Lord, the day she accepted Christ as her Savior, I never saw a happier person than her son, when he walked up and stood beside her. I began to see why You led me to that office. I felt so foolish about questioning Your leading.

Lord, forgive me for complaining about being the only Christian in that office. Now I know why I was there. I couldn't see it at first. I wanted to die every time they started talking ugly about You. But You know the funniest thing has happened. All the people in my office have stopped talking so ugly and stopped telling such filthy jokes. God, I haven't said a word about it to anybody, but I've noticed they never tell me a filthy joke. When I walk up and they're talking at the coffee machine or something, they don't say, "Here comes Ms. Goody Two Shoes." They say, "Come on and have some coffee with us -- that's about as strong a drink as you'll ever have." They laugh, and I laugh with them because I know You are using me in this secular office. I'm as much a missionary in the office as the missionary in South Africa. God, thank You for putting me here. I'm so sorry I griped about it and felt put out with You because you placed me here, but it has taught me a lesson. Christians are supposed to be in the world . . . not of the world . . . but in the world to spread Your love around. I'm so thrilled that's my job. I'm so thrilled that there are more here who need You as their Savior. I know You have a plan for their lives and I want help them find You. **Thank You, Lord, for letting me be in this place at such a special time. I love You Lord!**

I DON'T LOVE
You Anymore

Dear God,

Where did I go wrong? What happened to my dreams for the future? Never in a million years did I ever think I'd hear the words, "I don't love you anymore."

Many years ago when I was a young teenager I dreamed of growing up, going to college, marrying a wonderful Christian boy, having children, and just being a housewife. And I did just that. I loved dating in high school and college. In fact, I've always just loved boys. I'm so glad I'm a girl. Some people are miserable -- they haven't decided which way to go yet.

Well, dear God, I remember one Sunday morning when I asked You to come into my heart and give me eternal life. What a wonderful time that was. I've never doubted one minute that the Holy Spirit came to stay. He's certainly not a commuter. He doesn't come and go. He stays. I praise You for that.

And then I met HIM! From the beginning, I felt I had a future with him and he felt the same way. We really felt like You were blessing our relationship. We were married with all the usual fanfare that weddings cause. There was a honeymoon and then back to reality. I was so happy and I thought he was too. Three children came and altered our organized lives. I was caught up in formulas, diapers, and sleepless nights. I didn't realize that my husband was often eating alone, or fixing his own meals. I was surprised that he seemed preoccupied with the children, retreated into TV, or was always working. Communication seemed to break down. I felt alarmed, but couldn't reach him. The years passed. We neglected You . . . never talking to You as a family. I kept remembering my little girl dream, but found it fading as time passed. Then one day, out of the blue, I heard those words. The crying, pleading, and begging were to no avail.

God, I reached out to You in desperation. I had to change from a housewife into a career woman. A single parent. I hated it and complained to You and anyone who would listen. I had countless pity-parties with those familiar words, "Why me, God?"

I want to thank You for the day You jerked me out of my self-pity. You had helped me all along. You didn't leave me. So, instead of sitting in a pool of poor self-esteem, I began to count my blessings. First, those three wonderful kids who love You and love one another. Next, a host of friends You sent to sustain me. Then, my wonderful church that's so full of love. I became involved and found others in like circumstances whom I could encourage. I found out that great healing comes when we try to encourage and help others.

Oh, dear precious God, You gave me a scripture through this terrible time. I've clung to it and found it so true. You are so faithful. I get goosebumps everytime I think of it. Jeremiah 29: 11-12. **Thank you, precious God, for Your love and forgiveness . . . especially for Your mercy. Good night. See You in the morning.**

MEDDLING
Mother-In-Law

Dear God,

Being a mother-in-law is just about the hardest thing I've ever done in my life. I thought it was going to be so much fun, but I made a mistake when Jim and Nancy were first married. I thought they needed me to tell them everything. I mean, you know, what to do about the house, where to put things, and how to set up a kitchen. After all, being an interior decorator is my career and I thought surely my daughter-in-law would be thrilled for me to give her some pointers about beautiful things in the home and where to put them. They received such wonderful wedding gifts and they have a nice home. I was so excited, I just wanted to hop in there right away and help her. Well, I guess I stepped on her toes. I don't know what I did, but whatever it was, she began to say that she really didn't like that lamp here, or that picture there. She and Jim were going to decide what to do. My husband kept telling me to back off, but I felt like I knew a lot more about it all.

She couldn't even cook! Lord, You know she couldn't boil water! Nancy grew up with a maid in her home who had done all the cooking, so she didn't know her way around a kitchen. I'm a gourmet cook, and I was excited and ready to teach her how to cook because I wanted to help her.

Not long after they were married they went on a mini-vacation. I thought it would be so much fun to fill their refrigerator and freezer full of food. I had a key to their house and decided to have a meal all fixed and ready when they came home. I thought they would be so pleased, and besides that, it was a special day that they celebrate. I thought of everything . . . candlelight . . . a lovely table . . . a gourmet meal. I worked really hard and waited for them to get home from their trip. When they walked in the door, I have never seen anyone's face fall like hers! My son got real nervous, and I thought, "What did I do wrong?"

I said, "I thought it would be fun to surprise you with a candlelight dinner. They thanked me and smiled, but then Jim said, "Mom, this is our special night to spend by ourselves. It's one of those special nights we celebrate in our marriage. We had decided that we were going to go out to our favorite restaurant and have a romantic evening." Lord, You know who got their feelings hurt. Here I had worked all day long trying to make a surprise for them and they didn't even appreciate it! So I left, with my feelings hurt, which I know now was utterly stupid. I just wanted to do something special for them.

They made so many mistakes when they were first married. I just can't believe some of the mistakes they made! I remember at one of her wedding showers, Nancy told me she wanted me to be her best friend. I don't know what happened. I must have tried too hard to be a best friend because she started backing away from me. I kept thinking, "What did I do wrong?"

One day I got up the courage to go talk to her. Lord, You know how nervous was, because I asked You to help me say the right words. I prayed so hard that I would do and say the right thing. I knew I had to do something because Jim, our son, was in the middle, and that's a miserable place to be. I was trying to be the kind of mother-in-law that You would be proud of. I just wanted to keep them from making a lot of mistakes that my husband and I made. So, I went over to talk to her, and God, you know what happened, it didn't help a thing. I cried and said I was sorry for whatever I had done, and she said, "I don't want to be rude or anything, but you want us to be at your house every time we turn around. And, Mom, (she called me Mom for the first time, which kind of thrilled me) you drop in at all hours and we never know when you're coming. Sometimes you call when we're busy. When we ask if we can call you back, then we can tell that we've hurt your

feelings. I don't know how to be the right kind of daughter-in-law."
I thought to myself, "All she's doing is just telling me to back off."
Remember how mad I got, God? I came home and told my
husband what happened, and of course he said, "I told you so." But
I had to get things straight.

Time passed and we got past some of our
misunderstandings. But then the first baby came. Nancy's mother
was working and lives pretty far away, so she couldn't come. Well, I
said I would be glad to come and help. God, I couldn't believe what
they did! They didn't do things right at all. I know there are some
new ideas since I had Jim, but I just couldn't get over what they
would do. They would go out all the time, and when she was just
about to have the baby, she was still running all over town. They
went to a picnic -- I nearly died -- it was the day her baby was to be
born, and she went to a Memorial Day picnic! I thought the baby
would be born right between the potato salad and the barbecue! It
scared me to death and I begged them not to go. They just smiled,
patted me on the head, and went on. Of course, the baby didn't
come that day. It was born about a week later.

When the baby did come, I thought I would just walk in
and take care of things, after all I had done it all before. Everything's
different now, I kept wanting to do a certain thing for the baby, but
they would just let him cry. I wanted to pick him up, but they said
it would spoil him, so they let him cry. Jim would try to change
diapers, but he didn't know how to do anything like that! His father
had never changed his diaper, or given him a bottle. I always did
that. I couldn't believe how my little daughter-in-law not only
allowed him to do it, she told him to! He was trying, but he was
doing it wrong. I came to stay two weeks, but after ten days Nancy
was up and feeling better, and I decided it was time for me to go
home. Honestly, God, I think they were thrilled to death when I
said it was time for me to go. Lord, that child just gets into
everything. They're not raising him right. He's spoiled rotten, and I
keep telling them how to fix him. My husband says I need to stay
away and let them make their own mistakes.

God, I've had the worst time trying to figure out how to be a good mother-in-law. I've read every book there is (and they aren't easy to find). It seems like mother-in-laws have such a bad image. I really didn't want to be one of those mother-in-laws that people make jokes about. You know, God, Jim, Sr., talked to me at length the other night and told me I had really messed up as a mother-in-law. I decided I had better come talk to You. God, where do I stop and where do I start? I wish You would tell me. Oh, You have told me, is that what You're saying? You said in scripture that they have to have their own life? When we marry, the husband and wife cleave together and leave their mother and father. I know we leave physically, but I didn't think we had to leave emotionally. I guess You're right God. I wonder if there's anyway I can correct the mistakes I've made. I want to make it right, but I don't know what to do. Should I apologize again or should I just start acting like You want me to act?

As I'm sitting here talking to You, I am remembering my own mother-in-law. The more I talk to You, the more I remember the time when she lived next door to us. God, do You remember that? I used to get so sick of her dropping in all the time. I didn't realize that's what I've been doing. She would come over and try to help me cook, even though I thought I knew how to cook pretty well. I couldn't do anything to please her! I just said over and over again, "If I ever have a son, I'm not going to do that to his wife." God, I'm doing that very same thing! It's kind of frightening to think you can be so guilty of something and not even know it. I remember that we didn't even want to ask my mother-in-law to baby-sit our kids because she drove us all up the wall! She was determined to raise them because she lived so close. We didn't want her to baby-sit because she didn't have the same values we have.

As I talk to You, I am just sick about some of the things I've done. But I do know one thing, with You, it's never too late. I'm going to go to Nancy and tell her about my mother-in-law, and how she bugged me. I'm going to tell her I realize that I've been doing the very same thing to my own daughter-in-law, and how sorry I am. After that, I believe I know what my next step will be -- to bug off and back out! I'll let my children raise their children the way they want to, like my husband and I wanted to. If she never cooks anything that's really gourmet, what difference does it make? She certainly has made my son happy. He's gained about 50 pounds! She is such a sweet young woman, everybody loves her. She's so active down at the church, and she makes me so proud of her, but I know I've been negligent in telling her that. There were times I should have, but I was so angry, I wouldn't say anything. I want to have a great friendship with her so badly.

Then, miracles of all miracles, Lord. I cooked dinner for Nancy and Jim . . . my best gourmet meal. They just bragged and bragged, and I felt very comforted. Before I had a chance to tell her anything, she said to me, "You know, Mom, wouldn't it be nice if once in a while we could pray together?" Oh, God, I just died I was so excited. I said, "Oh, yes, let's do that, let's plan a time when we can set everything aside and pray together." To know that she wanted to do that after I've been so ugly, was such a blessing.

Oh Lord, please help me not to interfere anymore. Help me to give advice when it's asked for, and not before. Help me to know that she and Jim have to work out their own problems, especially their finances. I had been upset about their finances -- they weren't saving money like I thought they should. Me and my big mouth, You know, I said something about it. Jim put his arm around me and said so sweetly, "We'll take care of that, Mother." Inside I thought, "How unthoughtful -- they just don't appreciate my good advice." I'm sick of my advice, Lord. After I go over to Nancy's, and we have our prayer time together, God, help me to restore the relationship I almost ruined. Help me to be the kind of mother-in-law that she can love and talk sweetly about. Boy, I bet my hair would turn loose if I knew some of the things she's said about me through the years. Help me know how much to do, and what not to do. As I talk to You, I begin to see that maybe I'll just wait for her to ask for my advice. If she doesn't ask, I'll keep my little ideas to myself.

Lord, I don't know what I would do if I couldn't talk to You. It's so good for me to get these things off my heart and look at myself like You see me. I don't like the mother-in-law I've been so far, but I promise You, God, I'm going to be the mother-in-law that Nancy deserves. I love You, God. **Thank You for listening and helping me see what to do. I can't wait to talk to You again. I'm going to memorize Ephesians 5:31-33!**

SINGLE & LONELY

Dear God,

I'm single and lonely, feeling neglected and rejected. I'm tired of being "Aunt Jenny" to everyone in our family. I'm tired of being a baby-sitter for my sister's kids. She thinks I don't have very much to do -- what a laugh! I want a family of my own. I want to be a mom, not just an aunt. God, I've done everything I can think of to meet other singles. I've joined the choir, gone to single's classes, and attended city-wide single's meetings. They usually have 1500 in attendance and I'll bet 1,475 of them are there to meet "him" or "her." Is that motive all wrong? In my heart, I know it is. We're supposed to be there to praise You. I know I'm having a giant pity - party, but if I can get it out, then I'll feel better. I don't want to lay all this on my friends, even though a lot of them feel the same way. I guess at times I'm angry. No, "frustrated" is a nicer word.

So, the other night I decided to take stock of myself. I have a nice figure -- not sexy or sensuous, but attractive. My curly red hair and big green eyes are great (so I'm told). I have a great job, a company car, bonuses, a good salary, and I love my boss and co-workers. Mom says that men are threatened by me. What am I supposed to do? Give my car back and quit my job? I'm 34 and I've worked hard to get where I am.

I've dated quite a bit, but I absolutely refuse to compromise my values. So many of the people I know are living together and I'm amazed at how many of them are Christians! They rationalize by saying that You understand. I bet that hurts You.

Emotionally, I do have a little temper, but I'm working on it. Everyone says singles are selfish and self-centered, yet I know some who teach little children and teenagers. They are models of what You want. I really believe that if I can't back up my talk with my walk, then I'd better shut my mouth. I don't want to be selfish. I just want to be able to give my love away to a committed man who loves You too.

In my spiritual life, I know I love You and am committed to You. I want to know You better. I know that takes Bible Study and personal dialogue with You. We do have a good time, don't we, God?

Talking to You helps to ease my mind. You have been so faithful to bless me. Thank You, God. I know that You have a plan for my life, one that You designed even before I was born. It is better than I can imagine. I don't want this to be a "poor me" time with You. **I just needed to put this all writing so I could see how fortunate I really am. I am reminded of Psalm 139 -- how I love that Psalm. And I love You too.**

Psalm 139. My theme song.

FORGIVEN

Dear God,

I wonder why I struggle with feelings of guilt? I know we're not supposed to judge ourselves by the way we feel, because feelings go up and down. Still, I can't help but wonder why I feel this way. I know You forgive us of our sins because Your scripture says that You cast them as far from You as the East is from the West. I know that You have forgiven me. I know that Your Word says when You forgive, You also forget. But, God, I feel like Christians play a game -- unbelievers can't play it -- just Christians. It's called self-torture, and I've been playing this game a long time. My heart says, "God could never forgive me for the terrible sins I've committed," even though my mind knows better. Then I tell myself, "If You can't forgive me, then I have to punish myself."

You know, God, I think it goes back to when I was a young teenager and I accepted You as my Savior. I knew that I was born again and that You forgave me of my sins. I knew the Holy Spirit lived in me because I read that when you invite him in your heart, He stays there. I knew all of that, but as I grew older, I forgot about how important You should be in my life. And then, God, You know what I did, I kind of went off the deep end and I started drinking and even dabbled in drugs for a while. All the time, I knew that I was doing was wrong. I could feel the Holy Spirit nudging me and getting on me about it. God, I'm so glad You kept after me.

When I graduated from college and got a good job, I was very promiscuous and had an abortion. I'll never forget it as long as I live. I asked You to forgive me and I know You have. Yet I suffer with these feelings of guilt. Everytime I see a movie, or something on television about abortion, I get just sick at my stomach. I wonder, "Lord, did You really forgive me?" I know good and well You did, because Your Word says You are faithful and just to forgive us. Oh, Lord, I love You for promising to forgive me.

It was quite a while before I got my life straightened out, but I finally did. Everytime I stop and think about how much I love You and how excited I am to belong to You, then I know my doubts are not of You, they are of Satan. He reminds me of my sin. He says, "Look at what you did. Look at how you lived, even after you knew Jesus. Do you think that was right? How could you really be born again?" Satan has his holiday with me, but all the time that's happening, there's a still small voice inside me saying, "Don't pay any attention to him. You are born again. You are forgiven." God, after a while I feel free and joyful, I feel Your love and grace, and it just thrills me to death. But why do the feelings of guilt keep coming back when I know I have been forgiven? Lord, I know we can't ever erase anything from our memory. When something happens in our life, we always remember it, even after we accept the forgiveness You give us. I know that You don't grade sin like we do. In our eyes, adultery, murder, and stealing are the biggies, but we think the sins of gossip, criticism, and omission aren't too big. We act like we don't need to pay too much attention to the little ones. Man may grade sin, but I know that You don't. Any sin is separation from You.

God, when I get really down my mind focuses on the abortion I had, and I start beating myself up again. I know I'm forgiven if I've confessed my sin. You won't erase the memory of the abortion in my life, but You will erase the hurt, guilt, and those negative feelings I have so often. God, I've asked You to forgive me, but I've never really believed that You did! I didn't believe You could! I know You must be thinking, "What else can I do, but make her clean and good again, and help to her know it?" And so I'm asking You today, dear Jesus, with all the faith in the world, don't take away the memory, but please take away all the gook that goes along with it. Take away the sense of rebellion, and the feelings of unforgiveness that crawl all over me sometimes.

As I talked to You this morning, God, I'm so excited because for the first time I realize that You have already forgiven me. I'm playing that little game Christians play and I'm torturing myself, or letting Satan do it. At any rate, I'm making myself miserable. You've forgiven me! Oh God, that's so exciting, and today for the first time in years, I feel like it's real. I know that You love me and You have great plans for me. So many times when I've felt guilty about the past, I've thought, "How can I serve God and be effective for Him when I've done what I've done?" And then, Lord, Your sweet grace comes to the rescue. I know that if You waited for people without any sin to serve You, You probably wouldn't have very many people serving! You take what is left of our lives, whether we're young, old, or middle-age, and turn it into gifts. You don't call us to be successful, you call us to be faithful and consistent -- I know you'll do the rest.

I so much want to help somebody who is suffering like I have for so long. I want to help them see that You do love us. You forgive us -- period! That's exciting! I'm so thrilled this morning, God. I love You. I think of Ephesians 1:17 -- You forgive us with all grace. **This morning, I am beginning to understood that tremendous grace and forgiveness in a way I never have before. I love You, dear God.**

I WANT TO
Change You

Dear God,

I am so angry at people. How can You stand us? I don't know how in the world You put up with us -- we act so crazy. I guess I'm frustrated because I can't make everybody think like me. I'm angry at Elizabeth, my very best friend. For years You have been a part of both our lives. We accepted You at the same time and grew up together in the same church. We got married, and with our husbands, remained close friends. It's been wonderful.

Remember the crusade six months ago? You came into my heart a long time ago, but that night I gave You my life. I promised to get to know You better, not just superficially like I have in the past. You gave me a desire to really know You, and so I began to read Your Word. Oh how the scriptures came alive! All of a sudden, I understood more than I ever had before. Through everything I was learning, I began to be wonderfully aware of Your presence. It was more than a feeling. It was the sense that You are very active in all the areas of my life. The more I read and prayed, the more I wanted to read and pray! I used to say, "I'm going to sit down and pray for five minutes." Remember that Lord? I couldn't even pray for three minutes, I didn't have anything to say! Now, I can sit for 30 minutes, or almost an hour, and enjoy every bit of my time with You. I guess I'm really growing and it's exciting to me.

But, Elizabeth hasn't grown like that. She's just going along like we did before, and nodding to You at night and in the morning. Last night, I tried so hard to explain to her what had happened to me and how excited I am about my relationship with You. I wanted to tell her how alive the scriptures have become for me, and how I wanted that for her so badly. I told her how my life had changed and the joy I was finding in knowing You. All of a sudden I could feel tension. A wedge came between us like we have never experienced. I rattled on, but I began to feel sad. I went on and on about how I felt about You, and how it started at the crusade. I told her I wished that she could be close to You like I was. When I finally ran out of breath and stopped, she said, "Let me tell you something. You make me so angry I don't know to do. I'm thrilled to death that this has happened to you. I'm excited for you. If that's what you want, then great, I'm happy for you, but you're not going to push it on me. I want you to quit trying to be the Holy Spirit with me. Quit telling me what God wants me to do. If you really want me to tell you the truth, I'm tired of you acting like you know everything . . . like you just graduated from seminary. Even our other friends have said that you preach a sermon everytime you open your mouth. Don't you know that you can't make us have whatever it is you have? We have to find it for ourselves. I think you're becoming self-righteous and a little too proud of what's happening in your life, 'how close you're getting to God,' as you put it. I know you feel the distance between us, I feel it too. Maybe a day will come when I will experience God like you. But I certainly hope I don't forget what I was like before."

God, I was so angry with her, I couldn't believe what I was hearing! Self-righteous! How could she say that about me? My soul, I was just loving You, telling my friends about it, and wishing they had the same thing I have. Is that being self-righteous?

Well God, when I listen to You and stop focusing on my anger, I begin to see that I may have been pushy. Maybe I've been trying to push my friends into the wonderful experience I've had with You. Isn't that kind of normal, Lord? Isn't it normal to want to share something wonderful with everyone so they can have it too? Lord, Your Spirit is telling me, right as I'm speaking, that there are two ways I can demonstrate the love I have for You. One way is to be like I've been -- preaching everytime I see my friends and talking to them like I have something they don't. Lord, I'm sorry. I am so sorry. The other way to demonstrate Your love is to simply love them. Everytime I discover something new about You, then I love

You even more. If my love for You is real, then I'll love other people and get rid of the self-righteous attitude. My love should be sweet and sincere. I should be kind and forgiving. Lord, I want to be more like You. I want to be quiet and let Your Spirit work through me. Then one day, my friends will find the wonderful love I have found.

After last night I realize that I've been acting the way Elizabeth said. Lord, as hard as it was to hear, I thank You for her honesty. I know that I must ask her to forgive me for trying to be a preacher. Promise me Lord, that You will wink at me, or say something, to let me know when I do that again. If You'll do that for me and forgive me, I promise I'll stop acting like a self-righteous Christian. I'm going to ask Elizabeth to forgive me right after I get finished talking to You. With Your help, Your precious love will be evident in my life. I won't have to say anything -- they'll see it.

Lord, please help me not to forget this lesson. Our attitudes can do so much damage. Self-righteous Christians are one of the greatest stumbling blocks in the world. Lord, I remember in high school, I had a friend who was self-righteous and so legalistic. We weren't interested in You because of her! Help me to be the kind of turned-on Christian that can love You and show it to others. All this reminds me of I Peter 3:15, " . . . set apart Christ as Lord. Always be prepared to give an answer to everyone who asks you to give the reason for the hope that you have. But do this with gentleness and respect . . ." **I think I've been answering with self-righteousness. I'm going to ask Elizabeth to forgive me. I love You, God. Good night.**

THE OLDER Brother

Dear God,

You know I'm really feeling bad today. I'm feeling guilty, lonely, and angry. I'm feeling all those negative things and it makes me so mad. I just need to talk to you. God, I know my attitude isn't what it should be. I'm burned out and I'm sick and tired of taking care of my parents by myself. We all love our parents, but since my sisters live in different cities, and I'm right here, I am the sole caregiver. Once in a while, when I want to do something, I call them. They are both so busy with their own lives that they don't have time to come and help me.

I keep thinking about my sisters when we were younger. God, I know I shouldn't reminisce like this because it only makes me bitter. But I remember that during their high school days both of them nearly drove Mother and Daddy crazy. Emily is the oldest and I'm in the middle. Emily was into one thing after another. I remember seeing Mother and Daddy crying over Emily -- neither one of them knew what to do. They prayed so hard for God to give them some kind of insight about what to do with Emily. There was so much misery in our home during the time Emily was in high school and college. I swore that when I got older, I wasn't going to give Mother and Daddy that kind of trouble. Lord, I tried hard and I didn't do anything really bad. I didn't drink and I didn't run around with wild people. My parents seemed to be very happy with me. They told me time and again how much they appreciated me and how much they knew I loved them. I remembered how Emily had nearly driven them crazy, and decided I wasn't going to do that. When I finished school and got married, my husband and I settled in this town. By that time Emily had been married and divorced, and had two children..

While I was in college, my younger sister, Debbie, was in high school and she was a carbon-copy of Emily. I watched our parents grow old almost over night. I thought, "They just can't go through this again!" I tried to tell Debbie how Emily had kept our parents miserable and heart-sick most of the time. Debbie couldn't have cared less -- it was their problem, not hers. Debbie got into drugs and I watched my parents suffer again, just like they had with Emily.

God, I was so angry with both of my sisters then, and I still am now. They both live in other towns. Emily has two children and Debbie has three. A few years ago, I lost my husband. He was such a precious man. He helped me so much with my parents, but I lost him in death. We just have the one son and he is such a sweet guy -- he helps me out quite a bit. But God, I'm really mad today. I want to do some traveling, and now I've had to move in with my parents because they can't live alone anymore. They're not bed-ridden, but their health is failing. I feel like the "older brother." God, do You know what I'm talking about? I know You do. I know that I'm not supposed to be angry and inconvienced. I shouldn't be having a pity-party, I know that. But it doesn't matter now much I know in my head, I still seem to be doing it! All I can think about is the grief my sisters have brought to this family.

I am reminded of the story about the older brother in the book of Luke. The younger brother spent all of his money on wild parties and wild times, and then he came back home. His father loved him, forgave him, gave him his cloak, gave him a ring of ownership, and then said, "We're so glad you're home." I remember when I first read that, I thought, "That's the story of our family!" And then, the father had a party for the younger son and called all the people to come. That really hit me when I read it again tonight. The father killed the fatted calf because his son had come home. The father couldn't understand why his older son felt sorry for himself. He said, "Don't do that, don't pout. Come in and have fun with all the rest of us." I remember saying something similar to my parents, "Look at my sisters, they've gone off and spent all your money, worried you death, and driven you up the wall. Now when they call or come to see you, you just go crazy with excitement. I haven't done a thing except stay here and take care of you, and you don't seem to appreciate me." Lord, I feel so ugly when I say things like that. I know that Mother and Daddy love me and I know they appreciate everything I've done. I guess I feel sort of jealous that when Emily comes over, she's the center of attention. Her two kids are noisy, they don't mind anybody, and they're ill mannered. She takes off and then Debbie comes with her brood, and the same thing happens.

In Second Peter you tell us to "glorify you in everything that happens," and I'm trying real hard Lord. Well honestly, I'm not trying. I'm upset and angry. My parents are feeling terrible and I asked Debbie and Emily if they could please come and stay long enough for me to take a little trip with my son. Neither one of them could find the time to come. I know that You say, "Be angry and sin not." You say that we can be angry and not sin, but I'm angry and I'm sinning because of those two sisters of mine. I guess I'm angry at my parents, too, because they make excuses for my sisters. God, it seems unfair. Why won't they just come for a little while and share the load?

Well, I guess I'm just taking it all out on You, God, but I know You understand my heart. I know You understand that I am up to my eyebrows in feeling sorry for myself. I know I'm having a major pity-party. Lord, please help my attitude to be better. I kind of understand how the older brother felt toward his father for giving the younger brother a party. But I remember something else, God. I remember what the father said, "You have stayed home and taken care of everything, and your blessings will be far above any your brother could ever have." I will never have to look back with guilt or remorse for not caring for my parents. A part of the blessing is knowing that I have always tried to love my parents well.

Lord, as I get this off my chest to You, I'm already feeling better. I think I can go in there and be the sweet daughter that I ought to be. I want to stop talking badly about my sisters. Why can't I quit doing that God? Will You help me? Will You give me the ability to never say anything negative about Debbie or Emily? I want to love my parents and be the best I can to them. Lord, if I know You, You are probably making a way for me to have that week with my son. Then I'll be so ashamed for griping. Please forgive me, Lord.

Dear Jesus, as I talk to You, this burden has been lifted from my mind and heart. I feel sorry for my attitude. Please forgive me and help me to glorify You in all that I do. Some of my anger has subsided. Thank You for that God, because I was really angry when I first started talking to You. Help me, dear Lord, to be exactly what You want me to be, in everything that I do. **I love You, God, and in Your precious name I pray. Amen.**

FREEDOM
IN Grace

Dear God,

I'm still having a hard time understanding something. I keep hearing and reading about grace, but I'm having a difficult time understanding and accepting the idea of unconditional love or unmerited favor. So much of my life has been spent doing things for You. If I pleased You, then You'd love me. If I didn't do things for You, or displeased You, then I felt like You wouldn't love me anymore. Remember my home? I was raised in a home that taught if I was good and did good things, then I would be loved. If I wasn't good or did bad things, then I could lose my parent's love. My parents were never cruel to me, that's just how they were raised. So from them, I believed I must do good things to win Your love too.

The church I grew up in taught that I could lose my salvation. They taught me to believe that my salvation was secure as long as I did things for You. If I didn't do those good things, or "works," then Your love would be withdrawn. I didn't know anything about the security of my salvation. I thought I could lose it, work to get it back, and then lose it again! It always made me feel insecure and unstable.

I didn't realize exactly why I felt like that until my friend, Gail, asked me to come to church with her one day. I told her I already had a church home and told her how I felt about You. She kept asking me questions that bothered me, but she was so sweet and interested in me. She kept telling me that the Bible teaches that You died for us on the cross . . . You gave us grace and saved us. She would say things like, "The Bible doesn't teach that you can lose your salvation." Then Gail showed me John 3 where Jesus and Nicodemus were talking. Nicodemus asked Jesus how he could have eternal life, and Jesus answered, "You have to be born again." I got to thinking about being "born again" and then losing your salvation. I told her that it didn't make sense to me -- Jesus told Nicodemus you have to be born twice -- I thought we were just born once. Gail pointed out that we are born once physically, and once spiritually. Well, that made sense and the more we talked, the more sense it made. I didn't read anything about how good I had to be, or how many pluses I needed to have on my side to score enough for Jesus. I didn't ask Gail about it then, but I began to question all that I'd been taught. I will always be grateful to You, Lord, for my friend, Gail. She was truly your missionary to me.

Even though she asked me to visit her church a million times, I always said "no." She asked me for the millionth and one time. I told her again that I already had a church. But she kept on, and told me about a special program they were having. Well, I decided to go just once to satisfy her. She never asked me in a pushy way, and she never poured on the guilt, she was just sweet and caring. I went with her and heard this young man talk about the very chapter in John that Gail and I had discussed! I thought, "my soul," that's the chapter she and I have talked about so much. The preacher opened the scripture and talked about Jesus, and being born again. When he asked us to read the second verse, You began to tug at my heart, Lord. I will never forget how I felt. I thought, "I can't believe this. I can't go back on everything I've known my whole life." You know, God, that night at Gail's church, I began to feel like I wanted to know more, I needed to know more. I began to search. I searched my heart, but I didn't know enough about the scriptures to search them.

Gail and I were having lunch the next week and I told her how much I enjoyed the preacher at her church. I told her I hadn't really understood everything because at my church we have been taught differently. Her preacher said that when we accept Christ and He comes to live in our heart, He doesn't come and go. He never leaves us or forsakes us. Then Gail showed me a lot of other scriptures. One of them was Ephesians 2:8-9, "For it is by grace you have been saved, through faith -- and this not from yourselves, it is the gift of God -- not by works, so that no one can boast." I tell You Lord, I remember boasting about things I did for You and how proud I have been that I was being so good for You. I thought, "Oh, He must love me because I'm doing good things for Him." In my own mind I have been full of pride about what I've done for You. All of that seems so foolish now.

God, I thank You that Your Holy Spirit kept nudging me, until one day I asked Gail in a real shy voice, "Do you think it would be all right if I attend your church one Sunday morning with you?" She nearly fell out of the chair! She died laughing, "Would I mind? Could you come? Well, of course, you can and I'd be thrilled to pick you up!" That next Sunday, my heart was fluttering I was so nervous. I felt a little guilty for going against something I had been taught all my life, but I also felt a sense of searching -- a yearning to get things straight. When Sunday came, it was very exciting. I had never seen such joy in a church in all my life. My church is very quiet. We don't clap our hands or say "Amen" out loud, or do anything that would attract attention. We just sit and listen. Everyone sang the songs, and even though I didn't know them, I read the words up on screens. As we sang, Gail whispered to me that we were singing scriptures! I couldn't believe it. Everyone of those scriptures described how I felt. Lord, You were really speaking to me that morning. I enjoyed the singing and laughter. I couldn't believe that I was laughing in church. It was okay to laugh and have fun in church. We even clapped our hands while singing some of those choruses. Then all of the sudden they did something I had never seen before. The preacher told us to turn around and hug somebody and tell them you're glad to see them. I had about fifteen hugs in fifteen seconds, and I felt like I had about fifteen new friends!

The next week I waited until Friday afternoon before I told Gail I wanted to go back to church with her. She was so excited that I wanted to visit again. That Sunday, the preacher spoke right to my heart. There may have been thousands of people sitting there, but I was the one he was preaching to. At the end of his message, he said,

"If you want to ask Jesus Christ to come into your heart, come down to the front and talk to one of the ministers." Lord, I didn't mean to go down there, but before I knew what was happening, I was down in the front telling the minister I needed to ask Jesus Christ into my heart. We went into another room, and sat down and talked. He showed me some verses and explained how Jesus comes to live in our hearts and how He will never leave us. I was so excited! He asked me to pray and I knew something fabulous was happening to me spiritually. Then, oh God, his sweet prayer -- thanking You for saving me and giving me eternal life. That meant so much to me.

During this past year, I have never felt such love, contentment, and security. Every now and then that old record of insecurity starts playing in my mind. When it does, I go back to the scriptures and read about how much You love us, for free. We don't deserve it, but when we ask You to come into our lives, You do. I thank You that You live in my heart today. I thank You because I'm saved. I want to obey You and do things for You and be available to You, not to get my salvation, but just because I love You and You love me.

I'm free, dear Jesus, thank You, thank You, thank You, for the freedom of my salvation. I can go to sleep every night feeling peaceful and good. Thank You, God.

WHAT IS
Over the Hill?

Dear God,

Never in a million years would I have thought that I would be upset about being a grandmother. Since I was young, I have looked forward to getting married, having children, and eventually having grandchildren. But I didn't realize that at age 71, I'd feel like this! I've run out of energy, Lord. At church I'm always with a group of older people. We talk about what doctor we go to and what medicine we take. Lord, you know my vivid imagination -- I start feeling funny when I listen to what's ailing everybody else. I can hear somebody describing their symptoms, and by the next day I have it!

As long as I live, I'll never forget that time at the airport. I gave them my ticket and the agent asked if I was a senior citizen -- I was just 50 years old! It nearly killed me and it made me angry too! I pulled out my driver's license for her to see and indignantly said, "I am only 50 years old." She apologized and smiled and did everything she could to make me feel better. That was my first experience of knowing how it was going to feel to be a senior citizen. There are some nice things about it though. We can go to restaurants and get a 20% discount, or we get to eat cheaper than everyone else. It's not all bad! Then, there are the sweet ones who try to help us across the street, even if we don't want to go! Our precious kids are so wonderful about checking up on us, but when they start helping me out the door, that really gets under my skin! I don't want anybody helping me around, I can get along pretty well all by myself. It makes me feel so old.

God, this morning I do feel old! I know 71 isn't that old, but it's pretty old if you look at it realistically. My mother always told me the funniest thing, she said, "You know, it's not always bad getting old. It's not bad at all, because you can say what you think, or say something off key, or anything you want to, and they'll just smile back at you and say, 'Well, she's just old.'" That just nauseates me, Lord. But I've noticed it is true if you're not careful.

There's always something on television or in the newspaper about Alzheimer's disease -- how you get it, what to do if you think you have it -- so I read all that stuff and I'm going to quit it. Lord, You know me, I'll start thinking I have all the symptoms if I'm not careful!

Lord, I want to do something constructive in my church, I really do. I want to do something that will make a difference for You and Your kingdom. But they always put me on the prayer committee. I know that being a prayer partner is the sweetest thing in the world and it's the nicest compliment anybody could give you. Lord, You know I talk to You often. I'm glad they know I'm praying and talking to You. But Lord, maybe I could do something with little kids -- I think I have a lot to offer. I just can't seem to figure out where my niche is.

I have two close friends who are my age and the three of us get together for lunch about every other week. We talk about how we're feeling and whether we're feeling good or not so good, and what's going on in our lives. One of my friends is very optimistic, she thinks everything is going to be okay -- we're in the prime of our lives, and we're never going to get sick. The other one is so negative. She thinks we're all going to get cancer next week! She is always going to the doctor for checkups; she even dreams she has some disease and runs to the doctor to get a test. Then we get a blow by blow account of everything the doctor said. I can be so impatient with her and I feel bad about it.

Lord, was I born 20 years too early? Was I supposed to be born in another generation? At our church we have a contemporary service on Sunday nights. There's a lot of clapping, singing, hugging each other, and a whole lot of fun -- I just love it! I can't wait until Sunday night. I think it's so wonderful! Well, my positive friend says she likes it all right, she sees all the young people coming, and if we have lots of young people then that's good enough for her. But my little negative friend is about to have a fit -- she says it's not worship. I keep trying to point out to her that this is the way the young people worship. They worship just as much in their way as we do in ours. She disagrees because they clap their hands and jump around. She thinks the music is too loud and there is too much of it. As we sit in church together on Sunday nights, I keep pointing out to her all the young people, the teenagers, and young adults who are there. It's wonderful! I used to not want to clap when everybody else did because she didn't like it, but I just decided I would clap if I wanted to, and I did. I love the music. What's wrong with me, God? I think I belong with those kids. I may be 71 years old, but sometimes I feel like I'm about sixteen.

I want to be on the prayer committee because very little will happen in Your kingdom unless its backed up by prayer. I know it's an important place to be. But God, I want to do something else too. What can a 71 year-old lady do, who's physically fit and wants to make a mark in the world? I'm a grandma who wants to make some kind of a contribution to You and to Your work.

As I talk to You, I'm beginning to see that there is more to the prayer ministry than I realized. There is the ministry of presence -- just being there and loving people. I don't have to do something, I can just be there, listen and try to help when I can. I think young people want you to listen more than they want somebody telling them what to do. They need somebody to listen and from there, they'll figure out what to do. I'm a good listener, God. If You want me just to listen to those young people and to help them know You better, that's wonderful. Could that be what You're thinking about for me? Well, I tell You what, Lord, that would be exciting! I ask You with all my heart to help me be available when You have somebody You need me to listen to. I love You, Lord. I'm going to try real hard to be patient and wait to see what You have for me. Seventy-one is only a number -- it's not the end of everything or the beginning of anything -- it's just a number. My body is 71 years old but my mind is much younger. **Thank You for that God! I love You.**